THE MAKER'S PATH 📍
A BOOK OF STAVES

CHRIS BECK

©*Chief Beck*
All rights reserved.
2023

No part of this book may be used or reproduced by any means: graphic, electronic, or mechanical, including photocopying, recording, taping, or by any information storage retrieval system without the written permission of the author except in the case of brief quotations embodied in critical articles and reviews. Because of the dynamic nature of the Internet, any web addresses or links contained in this book may have changed since publication and may no longer be valid. Although every precaution has been taken to verify the accuracy of the information contained herein, the author and publisher assume no responsibility for any errors or omissions, so no liability is assumed for damages that may result from the use of the information contained within. The views expressed in this work are solely those of the author and do not necessarily reflect the publisher's opinions, whereby the publisher hereby disclaims any responsibility for them.

ATTRIBUTIONS
Interior Text Font: Minion Pro
Cover Design & Typesetting: Robbie W. Grayson III

BOOK PUBLISHER INFORMATION
ISBN: 979-8-8689-8495-2
Traitmarker Books
A Division of Traitmarker Media
www.traitmarkerbooks.com
traitmarker@gmail.com

Printed in the United States of America

Table of Contents

A Note from the Publisher (iv)

The Purpose of This Book (v)

I. A Book of Staves | 7

II. The Book of Canons | 34

III. On Energy | 49

IV. On Trust | 55

V. Before the Maker | 77

Epilogue

About the Author

Contact

A Note
from the Publisher

The publisher is not a medical provider, therapist, or first responder and is providing this book, *A Book of Staves* and its contents, on an "as is" basis and makes no representations or warranties of any kind with respect to this book or its contents and disclaims all such representations and warranties, including, but not limited to, warranties of mental healthcare for a particular purpose.

The content of this book is for informational purposes only and is not intended to diagnose, treat, cure, or prevent any life situation, mental condition, or disease. This book is not intended as a substitute for consultation with or treatment by a licensed practitioner. Please, consult with a physician or healthcare specialist regarding the suggestions and recommendations made in this book.

Traitmarker Books

The Purpose of This Book

A Book of Staves is a practice I put together in 2008 while deployed on a firebase in Afghanistan. It's made of several parts rooted in ancient practices.

A Book of Staves is a collection of thoughts we all have in common, for each of us has had these thoughts in one form or another. These thoughts need to be personally sorted out by each of us before we die or before the world ends—whichever comes first. These thoughts should be used as a guide for an individual or group to come closer to the peace and happiness that they and we all seek.

A Book of Staves is split into "staves." By definition, a stave is 1) a band of wood: a long, thin piece of wood, one of several sealed together to make the hull of a boat, or 2) a rung or bar of wood: a bar or strip of wood or other material, especially one that forms a rung in a ladder.

I offer you 26 staves with the hope that it builds your "boat" so that it floats better in the restless sea around you or lifts your "ladder" to a higher plane.

Next is *The Book of Canons,* which I derived from *The Book of the Dead,* from which I offer 13 canons. These canons are rules by which The Maker will judge us when we finish this life. However, wherever we breach a canon, there is room for redemption and healing if we are willing. Use these canons to reflect on your current behaviors.

On Energy includes observations I have made about what keeps us from making improvements toward peace in our personal lives. Seeing every thought and action as either low or high energy can help one cut through the bullshit of what keeps us stuck and makes peace elusive.

On Trust is a series of common truths and myths about trust, trusting, and trustworthiness. In my own life journey, I have experienced the difference between myth and reality, having been reared, raised, and trained in myth most of my life.

Before The Maker is a list of 18 mantras I have put together as a commitment to live according to ancient wisdom that is still relevant today, just as it has been since the beginning of human history.

I hope and pray for you, the reader, to consider your own path and make specific commitments to keep true to your Maker and yourself.

Chief Beck | New York

THE BOOK OF

STAVES

Written in Antiquity by unknown authors, compiled and passed on by word of mouth, etched on stone tablets, scribbled on papyrus, and blocked out on the Gutenberg Press.

Stave 1
Every individual has a spirit.

Look within yourself and see that spark, that thing that makes you a sentient being. The spirit is that piece of you that makes you an individual and creates your uniqueness. There is no man-made device to measure any quantity of your spirit, but you know it's there.

STAVE 2
Spirit is everlasting.

The spirit that is contained in your human form cannot be destroyed. It has the ability to grow and become more than it was. It achieves that through the experiences you give it while walking this planet. Treat it well, for you will be with it for a long time.

Stave 3
There is a Great Spirit, The Maker.

Many religions call the Great Spirit by many names like God, Lord, Allah, and Zeus. The Great Spirit resides in all things: the Earth, moon, stars, you, your neighbor, plants, and animals alike. To be close to the Great Spirit is to become close to everything.

When a person is at perfect peace with their surroundings, they are closest to the Great Spirit. When an individual flows, walks lightly, and has no quarrel with anything in life, they are at peace.

STAVE 4
The natural state of a human is happiness and peace.

A baby smiles, laughs, and plays when it is content. That is its natural state. A baby cries when hungry, cold, hurt, or afraid. But when all of these basic needs are met, the baby is happy.

When an adult has all of their needs met, they have the chance to be happy and then ultimately at peace. This is the natural state of humans and should be the chief end for all humans to achieve.

Stave 5
All humans are equal.

All humans have a spirit: all humans are the same in this respect. Each spirit has its own unique signature. These signatures incorporated into human form are also abilities or what we sometimes call *gifts*. The individual with one gift or ability is not superior to another who does not have that ability and vice versa.

Some signatures are not able to achieve peace by their very nature. Such signatures will cause strife within a social structure and will need intervention in one way or another.

In the end, we are all spirit. Treat each other with respect and reverence, for we are all part of the Great Spirit.

Stave 6
Your journey is yours, so walk it.

Your life on earth is your personal journey. Every step you take—forward, backward, or sideways—is your path.

Your path is only for you and you alone. Do not try to copy someone else's path or be fooled into thinking that someone else's path can dictate your journey. Of course, learn from others and try to do well, but they are not in your shoes, cannot walk your journey for you, or tell you that you are wrong in any way.

Stave 7
Let it go.

Trying to control the uncontrollable will only break you. Some things in life are just not yours to understand or control. Let it go.

Uncontrollable situations are like a cat. I don't understand what that cat is thinking or doing, and that is OK. Let it "go."

STAVE 8
No human has a better or superior connection to the Great Spirit.

Throughout history, some men have placed themselves above others by claiming a mystical connection to God. There is *no* special connection. There is *no* fast track or secret. There is *no* special human who wields power over you by means of a spiritual advantage.

We all have the ability to get closer to the Great Spirit, for we are all the same. Some humans in history have gained great amounts of knowledge in spirit and have gotten very close to a great peace. They are knowledgeable and should be learned from. But they are human all the same. Seek them out and learn from them, but do not think that you could not do the same.

Stave 9
Do not diminish another.

Church, mass, or any other name of a spiritual social gathering can be beneficial as long as it does not impede upon another individual's spirit in any way or at any time. It can be a great place to be with other spirits of like thought.

However, if attending these gatherings disturbs the peace of your neighbor next door, your neighbor 100 miles away, or your neighbors in another country, cease and desist. Your gathering and its rituals should not diminish *any* individual's peace or happiness anywhere at any time. By diminishing another, it interferes with the Great Spirit.

STAVE 10
There are four foundational questions.

There are only four questions you can ask that will tell you everything you need to know about an individual.

- *What's most important in life?*
- *Who's your hero?*
- *What are you most proud of?*
- *What is your goal in life?*

While there are hundreds of others, these four will allow you to understand another's foundation.

Stave 11

When a person is kicked out of a group for being different or for having different ideas, it makes you wonder if that group just kicked out Gandhi or Jesus, doesn't it? Group dynamics today will be the things of legendary mistakes in a decade or a century. History is a forever document. Try to be on the good side, and don't dismiss the outliers. That outlier might be the one who saves us all.

Stave 12

Praying in any form is just meditation and letting yourself know what your deepest desires are. Your prayers are not wasted as you are setting your mind and soul on a goal. The universe is always listening, so be careful what you ask or say toward a goal or a person.

Stave 13

There is no luck or magic: there are only opportunities. What you see as luck might have been 20 years of work that finally bore fruit. You may think it was bad luck, but you just weren't prepared and stumbled over something that should have been easy if only you had studied the terrain.

Stave 14

Good and bad are words applied to situations and outcomes, but they are only good and bad because we don't see the entire picture. Something you see as bad, like losing a job, might lead you into an amazing new career. Something as good as a gallon of ice cream… well, you get the idea.

Stave 15

It is better to have a beautiful soul than a beautiful body. Too many people work their whole lives on their bodies and are ugly inside. All of our bodies will become dirt, but our souls are forever. What will you spend your time improving?

Chief Beck

Stave 16

Sex is fun. Do it. Be happy.

Treat your spirit well while in this body, and be happy. If having sex with consenting individuals makes you happy, then do it. If it is not for you, then don't do it. Sex is not bad or evil unless it hurts another individual without consent. Not having sex will not bring you closer to the Great Spirit. Having great amounts of sex also will not bring you closer to the Great Spirit.

Obey social laws and customs. This makes sense and will keep you at peace with your neighbors. The age of consent and many other sexual acts have been debated throughout time and have changed with modern society and society at large. Obey the laws and stay in the flow society deems correct, especially in this area.

Sex is fun, so do it with consent and in private.

Stave 17

Gratitude is not only a gift to the person you are grateful for, but it is a gift to your soul that will blossom into your own gratefulness. It's a never-ending cycle. Be grateful as much as you can every moment, and you will see everything around you change, including yourself.

Stave 18

Your sixth sense is a gift from your ancestors to pay attention to what's going on around you. This gift might save your life, but you have to listen and stop talking so much to even hear it.

Stave 19

Every thought you have is what you become. Your feelings will attract good and bad. Your imagination will become your creations. So be careful what you think, and try to control how you feel. Always imagine greatness, because you are great.

Stave 20

When everyone around you is in a panic and you are calm, two things might happen. Either you will disappear and get away, or you will totally appear as the only leader in that chaos to solve the problem.

Stave 21

Encouraging someone to believe in themselves could be the moment you start the revolution and change the world.

Chief Beck

Stave 22

Have something in your life worth giving up everything for. (TCB—*taking care of business*)

Stave 23

If something is important and urgent, then do it NOW. If something is important but has no time limit, then do it when you make time for it—but write it down, don't forget it, and make the time soon. For things that are not important, it is wise to just let them go.

Stave 24

If you have more than three old good friends or family all meeting to do something, then GO and be with them. NO matter how much it costs in time or money, go meet them at that gathering. Too many times, we place value on money or time over friendships or family, and that is backward.

Stave 25

Beauty and strength are all relative to points of view. Truth and integrity are valued the same from all points of view.

STAVE 26
Love.

Love everyone and all creation as you would love God Who created everything.

How? Learn to love yourself. Look into your own eyes in the mirror and say three times, "I love you." If you live that love you are learning, others will see you and love will flow.

When love flows, God smiles.

THE BOOK OF

CANONS

*These are 13 basic rules adapted
from the Egyptian Book of the Dead.
These are the proclamations that you should
hope to say in front of The Maker.*

Chief Beck

Canon 1
I have not destroyed innocence.

Personal Reflection & Response

A BOOK OF STAVES

CANON 2
I have not stolen.

PERSONAL REFLECTION & RESPONSE

Chief Beck

Canon 3
I have not lied.

Personal Reflection & Response

A Book of Staves

Canon 4
I have not taken a parent from a child.

Personal Reflection & Response

Chief Beck

Canon 5
I have not attacked anyone.

Personal Reflection & Response

A Book of Staves

Canon 6
I have slandered no one.

PERSONAL REFLECTION & RESPONSE

Chief Beck

Canon 7
I have not been angry without just cause.

PERSONAL REFLECTION & RESPONSE

A Book of Staves

Canon 8
I have not polluted myself.

Personal Reflection & Response

Chief Beck

Canon 9
I have terrorized no one.

Personal Reflection & Response

A Book of Staves

Canon 10
*I have not shut my ears
to the words of truth.*

PERSONAL REFLECTION & RESPONSE

CHIEF BECK

CANON 11
I am not a person of violence.

PERSONAL REFLECTION & RESPONSE

A BOOK OF STAVES

CANON 12
I am not a disturber of the peace.

PERSONAL REFLECTION & RESPONSE

Chief Beck

Canon 13
*I have not acted or judged
with undue haste.*

PERSONAL REFLECTION & RESPONSE

---

*If you can at this moment recite all of these canons from
the Book of the Dead, then you are standing naked
in front of The Maker.*

On

ENERGY

*Life is energy: either low or high.
High energy moves toward peace.
Low energy moves toward
all manner of ill.*

Low Energy

The church (and other similar gatherings) began with a good idea, but then ego, greed, and a lust for power took over, corrupting the good with filth and substituting for it shells of hatred and discontent.

But there is a worldwide spiritual awakening that everyone senses, even though we also sense that we are spinning our wheels and that nothing feels like it's working. We are stuck in a state of demotivation, anger, and frustration.

That's because fear drives self-doubt, which turns into anger that demotivates you from pursuing peace and motivates you to achieve any number of misguided things to prove that you are worthy. You need to tap into the creative and loving life force.

Low Vibrations

- Fear
- Self-loathing/Self-hatred
- Jealousy
- Anger
- Hatred

High Vibrations

- Love
- Joy
- Peace
- Trust
- Faith
- Happiness
- Generosity

When Going Through the Low Vibration Detector on the Way to the Next Level

- Don't worry about taking *everyone* to the next level to build the boat and help everyone build it.

- You will get there by building your part and being at peace with yourself. Everyone else will catch up at some point.

- The journey is to the top. You will get there, and others will get there on their own time schedule. It might take longer for their path might be very different.

- Don't forget the New Covenant. Jesus was a carpenter and was good at building boats.

Individual Synergistic Raising the Vibrations of Others to the Higher Level

- When moving higher, sometimes you will stop. However, you will observe that you can *never* go backward. Sometimes, you plateau or hit a pothole or speed bump. That's a part of the process.

- The universe is expanding, and we are expanding. If you don't expand with it, then you are in danger of imploding and exploding at the same time. This is what I mean by *destruction.* So expand.

- Expanding can best be done through a mastermind alliance. Identify others on the path and join them.

GRADUATION DAY

- Everyone has done something great in the last few months. No matter what it is, they have graduated into a higher level. Acknowledge and celebrate it.

- You have graduated as well, and you are the valedictorian of being *you.* Put on your graduation cap and gown, come out in front, and give your valedictorian speech to all of us.

And those who were seen dancing were thought to be insane by those who couldn't hear the music.

NIETZSCHE

On

TRUST

Myths & Realities

*These are myths and realities about trust,
trusting, and trustworthiness.*

A Book of Staves

Myth 1
Trust is fluffy and soft.

CHIEF BECK

MYTH 2
Trust is integrity only.

A Book of Staves

Myth 3
Trusting people is risky.

Myth 4
Trust can be gained instantly.

A Book of Staves

Myth 5
You either have trust or you don't.

CHIEF BECK

MYTH 6
Once lost, you can't regain trust.

A Book of Staves

Myth 7
You can't teach how to build trust.

Reality 1
Trust is real and measurable.

Reality 2
Trust is character and competence.

Chief Beck

REALITY 3
Not trusting people is riskier than trusting them.

REALITY 4
Trust takes time and follow-through.

CHIEF BECK

REALITY 5
Trust can be built and destroyed.

A Book of Staves

Reality 6
Trust can be regained, but it's tough.

Chief Beck

Reality 7
When it comes to trust, we are all in class.

How to Build Trust

- Talk Straight
- Demonstrate Respect
- Create Transparency
- Right Wrongs
- Show Loyalty
- Deliver Results
- Get Better
- Confront Reality
- Clarify Expectations
- Practice Accountability
- Listen First
- Keep God, and Therefore, PEACE, First

Chief Beck

How Not to Build Trust

- Make Assumptions
- Cover Yourself
- Break Promises
- Shoot the Messenger
- Mix Messages
- Sugarcoat
- Demand Trust

How to Train the Body to Respond to Danger

When in sudden danger, the mind will tend to dissociate from the body by the fight-flight response. SEALS learn to control this response by training in highly realistic environments. One way anyone can train their body is ice water baths.

Fill a tub with water and ice cubes so that the water temperature drops between 35 and 45 degrees Fahrenheit. Get in the water and fight the impulse to leave or shiver.

Two things will happen. First, it involuntarily triggers the fear-of-death response from your body. Second, it trains your body to fight the fear of death by your figuring out the mind control mechanism to fight the impulse to escape the water or shiver. When you master this, you partially master your fight-flight response.

Chief Beck

How to Determine Objectives When Experiencing Danger

Avoidance never makes a problem go away. The military has an order of operation for dealing with problems: the OODA Loop (Observe, Orient, Decide, Act—repeat).

First, *observe* as much of the problem as calmly and quickly as possible.

Second, *orient* yourself to the maximum part of the threat that you can eliminate as quickly as possible.

Third, *decide* the best action to eliminate the threat.

Fourth, *act.*

Repeat. This technique is a loop, so expect to re-observe, re-orient, re-decide, and re-act if necessary.

How to Decide Who Comes First

Maslow's Hierarchy of Needs ranks needs:

1. The needs of the *individual*
2. The needs of *other persons*
3. The needs of a *group*

Taking care of your personal needs is the cornerstone of liberty and safety. If you're not safe, then you are unable to make others safe.

NIMBY (not in my backyard) says to take care of ourselves first and then others. Once you're secure, you then can look around and contribute to the safety of others. Even Jesus Christ said, "Love your neighbor as yourself." In other words, you can only love others *as well as* you love yourself.

So, never give up your ability to defend yourself first.

Chief Beck

How to Resolve Unhealthy Conflict

Resolving conflict with others is like being in a biker bar. Everyone in the tough biker bar is tough and carrying a gun, knife, brass knuckles, or other weapons. So, you can't be walking around the biker bar acting like a "tough" guy, because if one person fights then everyone fights.

If in conflict resolution you're aggressive, looking to find a solution for yourself, pushing only one narrative or a particular win, then everyone loses. This principle is true in diplomatic circles and even in war. If all you're trying to do in war is win, then everyone loses. Compromise is key. It isn't the dirty word it has been made out to be.

So if you're looking for a good time, you're going to find a good time. If you're looking for a bad time, you're going to find a bad time.

A Book of Staves

Poor conflict resolution is like playing chess or checkers in which there are strict rules to the movements you make, with the objective being to take out the most pieces (or checkmate the king). But in the game of GO, you are able to move in pretty much any direction and use countless strategies.* It's not about winning. It's about compromise. It's about dividing, isolating, and taking over.

---

*If an artificial intelligence (AI) were programmed with GO at its core function, it would be unstoppable.

Before

THE MAKER

The following are the values I choose to live by in order to do right by The Maker.

Value 1
Spirituality

Knowing that the universe has a Grand Designer and a Greater Purpose. Knowing that I am an integral part of that Purpose. Knowing that I am needed, that I am wanted, and that I am necessary.

Value 2
Love

Love is foundational and holds the entire universe together. Without God's love for us, we wouldn't be here. Without love for God, we would have no purpose. So, love is fundamental to every thought and action.

VALUE 3
Humility

Acknowledging that God is God of Everything and that every molecule in the universe and every unit of energy in your body is created by God. How can you not be humble?

VALUE 4
Bravery

Acting on any condition (including physical, mental, spiritual, or any other dimension) with integrity, even when unpopular.

Value 5
Gratitude

The greatest contributor to overall happiness. I must first be grateful for my own physical, mental, and spiritual well-being in all circumstances and at all times. Then, my gratitude will reflect on everyone around me.

Chief Beck

Value 6
Honesty

Speaking the truth and presenting oneself in a genuine way. The truth begins when you look in the mirror and tell yourself the truth. This is how you set yourself free.

VALUE 7
Kindness

Always giving from the heart without hope of compensation. Kindness is like butter. Everything is better with butter. Everything is better with kindness.

VALUE 8
Fairness

Creating opportunities for people to excel. Fairness is not the same as equality. Not everyone has the same ability or desire to be a football player or physics professor.

Value 9
Forgiveness

The key to happiness. You must forgive yourself as much as you forgive others. On a clean slate, anything can be written.

VALUE 10
Hope

The fuel of dreams. Without hope, the future is bleak. Dreams are the building blocks of the future.

Value 11
Quality

The Fibonacci sequence and Golden Ratio found in nature. True beauty is orienting ourselves to this value. Manipulating nature to a human value is the essence of ugliness.

Chief Beck

Value 12
Teamwork

Doing one's share in the most optimal and cohesive manner without being invited or told. The best team functions like a gear. No gear on a machine has to ask permission to do "gear" things. It just does.

Value 13
Love of Learning

Movement. Stagnation kills. A stagnant pond has no movement. A stagnant mind becomes death. You can learn from a fool just as much as you can learn from Einstein.

Value 14
Creativity

Ex nihil summa (from nothing something). Using the world around you in novel but beneficial ways. Creativity has two levels: innovation and invention. 99% of all creativity is innovation, because everything in the world has already been created (invented). Find the 1% and change the world.

VALUE 15
Perspective

Being able to provide wise counsel to others and having ways of looking at the world that make sense to oneself and others. If you are looking at one square inch of an elephant, depending on where it is, you could be looking at an ivory tusk or an asshole.

Chief Beck

Value 16
Judgment

Living according to the OODA Loop. *Judge not lest you be judged.* Always observe, orient, decide, act, *and* repeat. Thinking this way flows like water. Water doesn't say, "I'm going over there." It just finds its way over there. Judgment isn't like saying yes or no. It's like a whole bunch of maybes.

Value 17
Humor

The best medicine!

Value 18
Leadership

Encouraging a group of which one is a member to get things done while at the same time maintaining good relations within the group. All good leaders started out as followers. If you can't follow, then don't lead. Find a mentor and learn to follow.

Epilogue

I grew up Christian, then fell far away from that faith. I journeyed to the depths with Siddhartha, Nietzsche, Thor, and Jung. I searched my soul and found darkness until I found the light. The light exists only when you see and experience it yourself. No one can experience it for you. No one can lead you into it because it is within you, and only you can live it.

I was in Afghanistan on a firebase in 2008 when I wrote this book. Some of this you'll find in other sources in various forms. *A Book of Staves* is how I saw it and how it applied to me at the time. In death, I found the light of God. I see the fractal universe in its infinite design. The underlying code, the universal laws, and the matrix of life are all vibrations at a frequency within a specific medium.

There is so much more I'd like to share since my days in a futile 3D war. Until you've gone to hell, most people deny Heaven. I've been to both now, and I'm finally home. The journey continues...

About the Author

Chris Beck is a retired United States Navy SEAL who served for more than 20 years in the Special Operations Forces. Over the course of 13 deployments, he conducted special operations with small UAVs, HUMINT, and Direct Action missions. His final tours were with the Naval Special Warfare Development Group (DEVGRU or "SEAL Team Six") to head the Special Reconnaissance units and various Task Force missions as a HUMINT source handler and technical operations director.

In 2009, Beck was requested by name to be the Advisor to SOCOM's Science

Director, Mr. William Shepherd (SEAL/Astronaut). He became an integral part of SOF technology and advancements while serving in this capacity. In 2011, Beck retired.

Suffering from PTSD and other combat-related injuries, he was indoctrinated into the transgender lifestyle. A film by CNN was made in 2014 which partially portrayed the struggle Beck was facing in these tumultuous years.

While studying for his master's degree in Mental Health Counseling, he discovered, with great help from his wife Courtney, the true depth and reason for the transgender phenomenon. Having overcome the mental health crisis, Chris is living a fulfilling life dedicated to veterans through his nonprofit "Mindful Valor" while ministering his testimony of redemption and forgiveness through the grace of God.

CONTACT THE AUTHOR
www.chiefbeck.com

www.ingramcontent.com/pod-product-compliance
Lightning Source LLC
LaVergne TN
LVHW012054070526
838201LV00083B/4722